T0016006

BE MORE
TAYLOR

CONTENTS

INTRODUCTION

When 14-year-old Taylor Swift made her first demo, full of sweet, wholesome songs, she may have hoped to one day sing them in front of thousands of fans. Since then, she's surely achieved more than even her wildest dreams. Beyond the *Billboard* number ones and record-breaking tours, she has burrowed into the hearts of millions, to the point where her songs define whole eras of our lives.

Taylor's life and career have been a rollercoaster of love and success, with lows of heartbreak and criticism. She's come out the other side having learned many life lessons. No wonder that this sensitive and insightful lyricist would have so many words of wisdom that can help us with our own lives, whether it's navigating relationships, fears, identity, or our own creative pursuits. So read on to discover how you can be more Taylor.

DISCLAIMER
This book has not been written or endorsed by Taylor Swift. It was created for Swifties, by Swifties. It is a love letter to Taylor and all those who feel a connection to her.

CHAPTER 1

BELIEVE

IN LOVE

Love lights up our lives with glorious colors, whether that is passionate reds, optimistic golds, or Taylor's iconic blues. Love sometimes appears in unexpected forms and it doesn't always last forever, but it brings us together like nothing else. From first sparks to unhappy endings, Taylor can teach us much about love, in all its wonderful shades.

"No matter what love throws at you,
you have to believe in it. You have to believe
in love stories and Prince Charmings
and happily ever after."

NEVER STOP BELIEVING

Falling in love makes ordinary life extraordinary. It is like hearing the first notes of your favorite song: your heart races and you can't wait for what comes next. Everyday life becomes brighter and more colorful—whether you are taking the bus to school or hopping on a private jet to a stadium show in London, Paris, or Tokyo. Since the start of her career, Taylor Swift has brought this life, color, and sparkle into all her songs, whether they're about a person, a place, or the concept of love itself. Of course, we all grow up to realize that love isn't always a fairytale romance and Prince Charmings aren't always what they seem. The reality of love is bigger, broader, and much more unpredictable than a fantasy. Yet Taylor has never lost faith in the highest, truest ideals of love and neither should we.

"It's the most maddening, beautiful, magical, horrible, painful, wonderful, joyous thing in the world, love."

LOST LOVE IS STILL LOVE

If the path of true love ran smooth, Taylor wouldn't have been able to write hundreds of songs about its highs, lows, and times of total confusion. All of us Swifties have a favorite among her love songs, and it is often the ones about lost love that tug at our heartstrings most. We might not have all left a scarf at someone's sister's house and never got it back, but most of us know "All Too Well" what it is like to deal with a relationship being over and losing a bit of our heart along with it. Whenever you feel like crying yourself to sleep, take comfort in knowing that Taylor has absolutely been there, too. Heartbreak is the worst feeling in the world, but a playlist of #sadtaylorsongs will help you get through it. And when you're feeling better, which in time you will, "We Are Never Ever Getting Back Together" is the perfect cathartic karaoke choice.

"We're all hopeless romantics."

LOVE BRINGS US TOGETHER

When we talk about love, we often think about finding "the 1." It can leave anyone who isn't in a romantic relationship feeling like they are on the outside of a beautiful, glittering snowglobe looking in at a world they aren't a part of. But that's not the only type of love that bonds us. After all, what purer form of love is there than that between Taylor and the Swifties who have every one of her lines memorized, sing their hearts out at concerts, and even get lyrics tattooed on their skin? Unrequited love might sell records, but the two-way relationship with her fans is also one of the most important in Taylor's life. From inviting groups of lucky fans to her own home to spending an epic 13 hours signing autographs, Taylor really gives back the love and appreciation her fans show her. So don't be afraid to open up your heart in order to find your people—we're all hopeless romantics here.

"Playing mind games is for the chase ...
This is real life, not chess."

PLAY FAIR

Dating can be fun, but it can also be stressful. Imagine you are sitting around in Centennial Park, Nashville, and you start talking to someone with the cutest dimples. They just get you! Fast-forward a few months to your birthday party. It's past midnight and they haven't shown up yet. Obviously you're furious, but what do you do: spam social media with passive-aggressive posts or silently fume about it for the rest of time? As Tay herself says, "No one is a mind reader." Neither throwing tantrums nor acting like an unbothered cool girl will fix the situation. (And trashing their car with a golf club isn't a solution either ...) Whether it is to stress the importance of punctuality or break the relationship off entirely, you're going to have to speak up and say how you feel. One pro tip though: anyone who ruins your birthday doesn't deserve you.

"I was single and happy and carefree
and confused and didn't care."

LOVE YOURSELF FIRST

Although Tay has built a career on romantic songs and cites love as her biggest source of inspiration, she also knows there's more to life than having a partner. After all, being single for years at a time has never dampened Tay's creativity. When she moved to New York and began writing the songs that would become *1989*, Taylor embraced the freedom offered by life in the city and the opportunity to host lots of friend gatherings in her Cornelia Street apartment. Being unpartnered can also invite more strange, scary, exciting, incredible experiences into your life because you are liberated to do exactly what you love. If you want to travel the world wearing gold sequined outfits—do it! If you want to head home to the cats and do some embroidery, that is just as awesome. You do you.

CHAPTER 2

FIND YOUR

PEOPLE

Taylor wasn't always the popular kid at school. She knows what it's like to sit alone, so now she holds her friends close and makes sure to save them a seat at her table. Her troubles with friends have made headlines, but behind the scenes, Tay has learned what it takes to help a friendship go the distance.

"Loyalty is probably the most important character trait."

STAND BY YOUR PEOPLE

Few of us have to deal with the pressure that being one of the world's most famous people puts on friendships. Gossip magazines will pay for your secrets, people might try and befriend you to take advantage of your wealth, and peers could even leak your private phone calls online in an attempt to get you canceled. We all deserve friends who we can trust. If your friend is going through their own personal *reputation* era and it feels like the whole world is against them, your support can make all the difference. Taylor considers herself fortunate to have been surrounded by true ride-or-die friends over the years. And that loyalty goes both ways. As Ed Sheeran once said, "She would be there if everything ended for me ... Taylor is kind of an anomaly in that sense."

"One thing about learning to be the best friend you can possibly be is knowing when to let people figure things out on their own."

RESERVE JUDGMENT

There's a fine line between unconditionally supporting your friends and not letting them do stupid things. Finding this balance can take time, practice, and patience. Of course, Tay is human, so there have been times where she has been caught rolling her eyes or sticking out her tongue when one of her friend's exes is seen or talked about in her vicinity. But generally, Taylor has exhibited saintly patience with her friends' dating choices (even going on cozy boat rides with her ex-bf Joe Jonas and her bff Gigi Hadid when the pair coupled up ...). As tempting as it is to judge your friends' decisions—in love, fashion, career, or anything else—the kinder thing to do is to let them be. Help them make safe choices, but don't dictate to them what you think is "right" or "wrong." Remember, one day you'll dip your toe in treacherous waters yourself. And the last thing you want to hear while crying on a friend's shoulder is, "I told you so."

"Other women who are killing it should motivate you, thrill you, challenge you, and inspire you."

RAISE EACH OTHER UP

The music industry, and society in general, can often try
and create rivalries between people. This can create the
impression that someone else's success equates to our
own failure. But that's simply not true. When you surround
yourself with people you think are awesome, it actually
reflects back on you! When Taylor brought out special
guests on the *1989* tour, including Lorde, Idina Menzel,
Mary J. Blige, and Joan Baez, she demonstrated that
she was more than happy to share the stage. And when she
was crowned 2019 *Billboard* Woman of the Decade, Taylor
made a point of shouting out other women in the industry,
from rap bombshell Megan Thee Stallion to songwriter
Tayla Parx, all deserving of their own crowns. Life is a
collaboration, not a competition. We all need a cheerleader
to encourage us to achieve our goals. If you can be that
person for others, you're winning, too!

"Apologizing when you have hurt
someone who really matters to you
takes nothing away from you."

SAY SORRY

Friendships are one of life's most fun and rewarding relationships. But while friendship should be 90% silliness, eating pasta, and doing karaoke together, there's 10% that isn't always so easy. One of the hardest things to face up to is when you hurt someone else. We all tend to think of ourselves as the main character in our life, so when we get into conflict, it can be tempting to cast the other person as a villain. Even when we know we're in the wrong, we might feel too awkward and ashamed to apologize. Take a tip from Katy Perry this time. The drama around "Bad Blood" made a reconciliation between Taylor and Katy seem impossible at one point—that's until Katy sent Taylor an actual olive branch as a way of saying "Can we move past this?" This message of peace opened the door, and soon this pair of pop icons were ready to hug it out ... dressed as a burger and fries, naturally.

"This is not about me."

BE AN ALLY

Part of being a good friend, family member, and citizen is standing up for and championing others. When Taylor stated her support for the LGBTQ+ community in the video for "You Need to Calm Down," her fame meant that the message reached millions of people around the world. Importantly, Taylor also encouraged her fans to take concrete action and sign a petition to support equality legislation. Some people didn't like this message and threatened to boycott her music. Others were critical, not because they disagreed, but because they thought Taylor had waited too long to speak. But being a good ally isn't about getting praised or being universally liked. It isn't about you at all. It's about listening, learning, and doing what you can do to support others—through your words and your actions.

CHAPTER 3

CONQUER

YOUR FEARS

Imagine yourself on a stage. There are thousands of fans screaming, waiting for you to perform. The eyes of the world are upon you. How do you feel? Taylor faces this pressure every night on tour, sometimes with nothing but her guitar for support. There's often been professional and personal challenges waiting offstage, too. So let's channel some Tay vibes and learn how to embrace our emotions, even tricky ones.

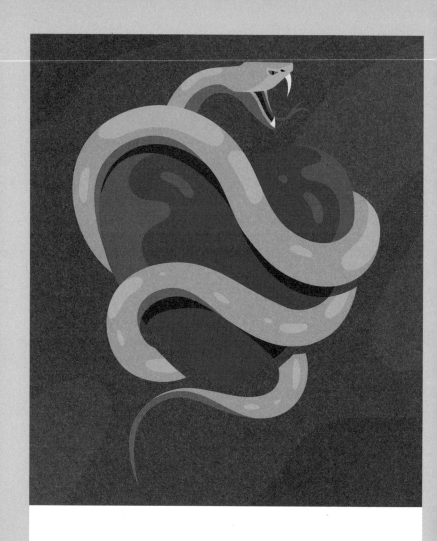

"The only real risk is being too afraid
to take a risk at all."

ANXIETY WILL NOT BEAT YOU

Anxiety is a very normal reaction to the tough things life throws at us. It can come in the moments before we have to make a big presentation or after a party as we lie awake wondering why no one laughed at our joke. It can be the result of being bitten by a situation one too many times before. Managing anxiety isn't about being totally fearless in every situation, but it is important not to let fear rule you. If Taylor feared performing in front of a crowd, she never would have moved to Nashville. If she feared public or critical reactions, she might not have dared take on the venture capitalists and rerecord her albums. And if Taylor Alison Swift let fear rule her heart, she would have never introduced herself to a certain curly-haired boyband member, resulting in an incalculable loss to pop music. Your worst fear might come true. But what if something great happened instead?

"You have to recalibrate and reassess your relationship with social media."

STEP BACK FROM SOCIALS

The version of the world we see through our phone screens can increase our fears of being left out; being judged; or not being as pretty, successful, and fun as other people. Taylor has experienced the best and worst of social media over the years, from directly interacting with fans on Tumblr (iconic) to her Instagram being infested with cruel snake emojis. She's therefore had to take some fairly extreme steps to make social media work for her. Who can forget her famous "there will be no explanation, only reputation" vow of silence? For those of us without 170+ million Instagram followers, having comments turned off and following zero people would probably defeat the purpose of social media. However, there are things we can all do to make the internet a less scary place. Monitor your screen time, curate your feeds to avoid unhelpful comparisons, keep some things private, and avoid the trolls who lurk in the comments section.

"In life, you can't get everything right. A lot of times you make the wrong call, make the wrong decision. Say the wrong thing."

FORGIVE YOUR MISTAKES

Part of suffering from Good Girl Syndrome, otherwise known as perfectionism, is a fear that one mistake will ruin everything. Everything can include your job, your relationships, and even your sense of self. So when you do make a mistake, which you inevitably will because we're all human, it can feel devastating. At times when Taylor's "perfect" image has slipped, a lot of people gloated that her so-called fakeness had finally been revealed. But what if we let her be more complex than simply a "good" or "bad" girl? She's sweet, goofy, and funny, but also business-minded, strategic, and stubborn. Women in pop are treated as two-dimensional objects when in fact they're mirrorballs, shining in a hundred different directions. In a way, it's liberating to let the mirror shatter sometimes. Next time you make a mistake, apologize if you need to, but don't berate yourself forever. No one is perfect.

"A lot of the best things I ever did creatively were things that I had to really fight—and I mean aggressively fight—to have happen."

CONFLICT IS OKAY

As scary as it might seem, sometimes we have to fight to do brave and exciting things. When Taylor started working on *Red* after three successful country-pop albums, she had to argue with the executives at her record company for the chance to work with pure-pop producers like the legendary Max Martin. She didn't just have one difficult conversation, she had the same argument over and over, but she didn't back down. She eventually persuaded them to let her try something new, and the rest is history. Years later, Taylor refused to let her music feature on streaming services until the companies offered better terms to musicians. This time, she was also fighting on behalf of smaller artists who weren't in a position to advocate for themselves. Disapproval or disappointment from people in authority can feel like the worst thing in the world, especially if it comes from people you love or respect. But if you never get into any conflict, how will you ever grow?

"Grow a backbone, trust your gut, and know when to strike back."

BE KIND, BUT BE TOUGH

Taylor says she was raised to be "a polite young lady."
Being polite is a great thing—especially if the alternative
is being a megastar diva who is famous for their temper
tantrums. But where do you draw the line between being
kind to people and letting them walk all over you? If you are
afraid to vocalize your needs or say "no" to people, you risk
people taking advantage of your politeness. It can happen
with friends, loved ones, or even in the workplace.
Of course, there's not always anything you can do about it.
Some people are just mean. Other times, you can stop
people inadvertantly steamrolling over your feelings by
standing up for yourself. Setting boundaries is important
because it helps everyone know where they stand. Be fair to
yourself by figuring out what you want, and fair to others by
letting them know when they've hurt you. Maybe just tell
them directly rather than writing a song about it though ...

CHAPTER 4

BE EXTREMELY

YOURSELF

When you are a fan of someone, it can be tempting to try and become just like them.
But when you look past the sparkles to the real Taylor, you realize that she's not asking for everyone to be exactly like her. The message of her music is to get in touch with your own true self.
That could take any form. Your only job is to figure out who *you* truly are.

You are your own definition of beautiful and worthwhile.

BE YOURSELF ... SERIOUSLY

The advice to "be yourself" is one of the world's most famous clichés. Annoyingly, it's also one of the most profoundly true pieces of advice you'll ever receive. Many of us try on different looks, personas, and ways of talking to make ourselves more popular or palatable to others. Not only is pretending to be someone else exhausting, it means that any success you have isn't really your own. In the lyrics of "Delicate," Taylor is surprised and happy to be liked for who she is, even though her America's Sweetheart persona has seemingly come crumbling down. Being loved for her true self (even if that's a cat-obsessed woman whisper-shouting lyrics into her phone at 2 a.m.) lets her break down the walls that were both protecting her and holding her back.

"You've got to allow yourself that grace to put on a certain lifestyle, or a certain outfit, or a certain creative mantra, then discard it when you outgrow it."

GROWTH IS GOOD

Choices that are right for the time don't have to be right forever. Taylor's Fourth of July party used to be a staple of the celebrity social calendar. A number of Taylor's friends, including Blake Lively, Cara Delevingne, and Ed Sheeran, would descend on her Rhode Island house in coordinating red, white, and blue outfits. Every year, the "Taymerica" celebrations got bigger and more Instagram-friendly, peaking with an inflatable slide and fireworks. Then the parties stopped. According to Taylor, she realized that making a big show of having so many friends actually alienated others, and she started to feel uncomfortable with unexamined patriotism in a time of political upheaval. It doesn't mean the parties were wrong, they just ran their course. If there is something in your own life that you doesn't fit you anymore, it's okay to put it aside. Making new friends, reinventing your wardrobe, or giving up a hobby doesn't mean you are a "quitter" or a "fake," it just means you're growing.

"Music is the only thing that's ever fit
me like that little black dress you wear
every single time you go out."

FIND YOUR PASSION

Some people are good at absolutely everything.
I know you're thinking of that one overachiever from school
with 15 extracurricular activities and perfect grades.
Whether it's becoming an Olympic gymnast or a rocket
scientist, it seems like those people can literally do
anything they set their mind to. For most of us though, we
have one or two things we are really good at and that's
more than enough. For Taylor, her natural talents and clear
passion for music help her make being a popstar look easy.
(Although a lot of hard work and perserverance is definitely
involved, too!) It's worth trying out as many experiences,
activities, and types of work as you can to see where your
own natural interests lie. There can only be one Taylor
Swift, but maybe you could be the Taylor Swift
of skateboarding or pet grooming.

"I'm always going to care.

There's never going to be
a time where I'm going
to be nonchalant or casual."

T.S.

CARE DEEPLY

Being sensitive is a gift. It is what connects us with the world and the people we share it with. It is the reason Taylor's lyrics speak so perfectly to the feelings of joy, sadness, anger, wonder, and doubt that we all experience. However, on our worst days, having a lot of feelings can feel like a curse. In those moments, breakup bops like "Better Than Revenge" are all too relatable, but they can also be kind of mean-spirited. The answer isn't to cut yourself off from ever caring again though. Next time your feelings are hurt, channel the message of "Happiness" instead. Here, Taylor stops herself from going down the road toward jealousy and bitterness and looks to a more positive future. She embraces her feelings but doesn't let negativity overwhelm her.

"With every reinvention, I never wanted to tear down my house. 'Cause I built this house."

STAY TRUE TO YOURSELF

With the standard for reinvention set by icons like Madonna and Lady Gaga, there's an expectation that every two years we'll get a "new" Taylor, creating a distinctive new era we can recognize from just a single image. Taylor even playfully called back to her previous personas, with a whole line-up of her past selves in the video for "Look What You Made Me Do." Over the years, Taylor has dramatically changed her hair, from loose country curls to the blunt white-blonde Bleachella bob, and even her accent, losing the specific twang that defines country music. Underneath all the superficial changes are certain things that have always been recognizably Taylor though, from a classic red lip to her outstanding commitment to referencing the color blue in her lyrics. More recently, the more gentle evolution between sister albums *folklore* and *evermore* shows that, while reinvention can be fun, there's no need to change just for the sake of it.

CHAPTER 5

CREATE YOUR

OWN FOLKLORE

If there is one single thing Taylor loves to talk about the most, even more than her cats, it is songwriting. Music is infinitely interesting to her because there's always a different melody to find or a new story to tell. You can't conjure love, friendship, or a record deal into your life, but you can always be creative.

October 2014
New York City

"If you just start to write in your free time and you make writing something that you look forward to, who knows where it will take you ...

There are so many different things that you can discover about yourself if you write."

T.S.

PUT PEN TO PAPER

Even when you don't feel like sharing your thoughts with anyone in the world, you can share them with the page. All you need is a notebook and a safe place to keep it. (And it's just for you, so don't worry about spelling or having beautiful handwriting!) Not only is journaling soothing and creative, it is also an incredible way to preserve exact moments in your life before you forget all the little details of people, places, and how you felt at the time. It can also shape your career! Taylor has been writing in her diary since she was a child, and this tradition has helped her become the remarkable lyricist she is today. Whether your thoughts stay strictly for your eyes only or you one day share them with the world, you'll always be grateful to be able to look back and remember the details of the unique and magical story that is your life.

"You have to write 100 songs before
you write the first good one."

KEEP TRYING

Many of us get disheartened if we don't think we are good at something on our first try. Then the fears and doubts can start to creep in. What if you write your first song, or first short story, and the people you share it with don't like it? Or you put your artwork online and everyone ignores you? When your creative endeavors aren't an instant success, the temptation to quit can be strong. Creativity isn't an overnight thing though. The world's most successful artists have more than just talent, they have persistence. Whether you want to be a painter, a writer, a dancer, or anything else creative—keep practicing. If the first thing you make doesn't resonate with people, that doesn't mean the next thing won't. Eventually, you'll find a particular turn of phrase or take a photograph that does connect with someone. Every single person you admire has failed at some point. They never gave up, and neither should you.

"Enthusiasm can protect you from anything. You can come back, even if you have a failure, you're rejected or criticized for something, you can become enthusiastic about the next thing."

DO WHAT YOU LOVE

It's easy to look at Taylor's three* Grammys for Album Of The Year as evidence that she's universally admired. Yet, unbelievable as it may seem, there are some people out there who don't like Taylor's music and find her very existence annoying ... bizarre. That's why you should never let other people dampen your excitement for a creative project you feel passionate about. Taylor always finds a way to channel her boundless enthusiasm and appetite for fun into her work, sometimes in unexpected ways. Did you know that when she first invited Ed Sheeran to her house, they wrote "Everything Has Changed" while bouncing on a trampoline? Happiness is the highest good: if you do things that you love, even if almost everyone else hates it, you're ultimately the winner.

*so far

"I wanna love glitter and also stand up for
the double standards that exist in our society.
I wanna wear pink and tell you how I feel about
politics and I don't think that those things have
to cancel each other out."

WORDS HAVE POWER

Taylor built her fame and success on her emotional but sparkling pop tunes. The genre and subject matter of her songs has meant that some "serious music fans" (people who like rock music) have dismissed Taylor as being shallow, lacking in talent, or being empty-headed.

But those songs speak to a huge amount of other people, particularly those who know how tough it can be to navigate a world that discriminates against people for their gender or sexuality. As Taylor explored in "The Man," women often get judged more harshly for their behavior and given less credit for their work. Taylor chose to use her words to spread the message that everyone deserves to be treated with equal respect, whether they're wearing a pinstripe suit or a glittery catsuit. Always remember, being creative can be fun and personally fulfilling, but you can also use your art to make a difference in the world.

"Have a sharp pen, and a thin skin,
and an open heart."

FEEL IT ALL

Taylor has come a long way since she was a teenager writing songs in her bedroom and dreaming of stardom. Yet, in many ways, she's still that same girl. No matter how big a star Taylor becomes, she has never lost what made her a success in the first place: emotional openness. When we search for the wonderful things in life—like love, friendship, and creativity—we also risk disappointment, rejection, and heartache. But the answer isn't to put up walls and try to stop yourself from feeling anything at all. When you're feeling angry, try and write some sassy lyrics about your ex in your journal. When you're sad, put on headphones and listen to *evermore*. And when you're feeling on top of the world, dance to "Shake It Off" like no one is watching. Whatever it takes, be a little more vulnerable, a little more Taylor, and a little more you.

Project Editor Beth Davies
Designer Isabelle Merry
Senior Production Editor Jennifer Murray
Senior Production Controller Louise Minihane
Managing Editor Pete Jorgensen
Managing Art Editor Jo Connor
Publishing Director Mark Searle

Written by Kitty Layton
Cover and interior illustrations Nastka Drabot
Additional artwork Isabelle Merry

DK would like to thank Satu Hämeenaho-Fox for her contributions to this book, Victoria Armstrong for editorial assistance, and Kayla Dugger for proofreading.

Quotations: **p.6** *Fearless* (album liner notes), 2008; **p.8** *Vogue* (video interview), 2012; **p.10** *The New Yorker* (interview), 2011; **p.12** *Elle* (article), 2019; **p.14** *Vanity Fair* (interview), 2013; **p.18** Apple Music (video interview), 2020; **p.19** *Rolling Stone* (interview), 2017; **p.20** 2DayFMSydney (video interview), 2014; **p.22** *TIME* (interview), 2014; **p.24** *Elle* (article), 2019; **p.26** To Apple, Love Taylor (open letter), 2015; **p.30** *The Wall Street Journal* (article), 2014; **p.32** The Taylor Swift Interview–Zane Lowe (radio interview), 2019; **p.34** *Rolling Stone* (interview), 2019; **p.36** *Miss Americana* (documentary), 2020; **p.38** *Elle* (article), 2019; **p.42** *1989* tour (speech), 2015; **p.44** Apple Music (video interview), 2020; **p.46** *Esquire* (interview), 2014; **p.48** *The New York Times* (interview), 2010; **p.50** *Vogue*, (interview), 2019; **p.54** Scholastic: Open A World of Possible (web chat), 2014; **p.56** *Vanity Fair* (interview), 2013; **p.58** Radio 1's Live Lounge (interview), 2014; **p.60** *Miss Americana* (documentary), 2020; **p.62** *Miss Americana* (documentary), 2020.

First American Edition, 2022
Published in the United States by DK Publishing
1745 Broadway, 20th floor, New York, NY 10019

Copyright © 2022 Dorling Kindersley Limited
DK, a Division of Penguin Random House LLC
24 25 26 10 9 8 7
014–328661–Mar/2022

A catalog record for this book
is available from the Library of Congress.
ISBN 978-0-7440-5792-8

DK books are available at special discounts when purchased in bulk for sales promotions, premiums, fund-raising, or educational use. For details, contact:
DK Publishing Special Markets, 1745 Broadway, 20th floor, New York, NY 10019

SpecialSales@dk.com

Printed and bound in Canada

www.dk.com

MIX
Paper | Supporting
responsible forestry
FSC™ C018179
www.fsc.org

This book was made with Forest Stewardship Council™ certified paper – one small step in DK's commitment to a sustainable future.
Learn more at www.dk.com/uk/ information/sustainability